To Our
Cuzino Grandsons
Love
Grandma & Grandpa

What Do You Think?

The Book of PROBLEM SOLVING

Jack and Selma Wassermann
Illustrated by Dennis Smith

WALKER AND COMPANY · NEW YORK

First published in the United States of America in 1990
by Walker Publishing Company, Inc.

Library of Congress Cataloging-in-Publication Data

Wassermann, Jack.
The book of problem solving / Jack and Selma Wassermann :
illustrated by Dennis Smith.
p.   cm. — (KidSkills)
Summary: Introduces the skill of problem solving and challenges
the reader to practice and master it as a part of thinking
critically and creatively.
ISBN 0-8027-6953-3 : — ISBN 0-8027-6954-3 (lib. bdg.) :
1. Thought and thinking—Study and teaching (Primary)—Juvenile
literature.   2. Reasoning—Study and teaching (Primary)—Juvenile
literature.   3. Problem solving—Juvenile literature.   [1. Problem
solving.   2. Reasoning.   3. Thought and thinking.]   I. Wassermann,
Selma.   II. Smith, Dennis, ill.   III. Title.   IV. Series:
Wassermann, Jack.   KidSkills.
LB1590.3.W378   1990
370.15'24—dc20   89-78176
CIP
AC

Printed in the United States of America

Sarah has a problem.

Sarah's cat has had her kittens.
But Sarah's cat Muffin has **hidden** her kittens.
That is Sarah's problem.

Sarah knows the kittens are not in the house.
She has looked from top to bottom and side to side.
There are no kittens in the house.

"How am I going to solve this problem!" cries Sarah.

Here comes Wanda.
She asks Sarah, "Did Muffin have her kittens?"
"Yes," says Sarah. "Muffin has had her kittens.
But I can't find them."

"You've got a problem," Wanda says.

"But I have an idea. Muffin will have to feed her kittens soon. We will follow her and she will show us where her kittens are."

Here comes Chico.
"Did Muffin have her kittens yet?" he asks.
Wanda tells him Muffin had her kittens but Sarah has a problem.
"She doesn't know where to find them."

Chico has an idea.
"Kittens make a lot of little meows.
Let's walk around very, very quietly.
We can listen and hear where the kittens are.
Maybe that will solve your problem."

Here comes Annabel.
"Come help us solve Sarah's problem," calls Chico.
"Muffin had her kittens but we don't know where to find them."

"I have an idea," says Annabel.
"There are four of us here.
If we each go to a different part of the yard and look for them
we might see where they are."

Finding Muffin's kittens is a problem.
But Wanda, Chico, and Annabel all have good ideas for solving it.
Which idea is the best?

What do YOU think?

Maybe you have a better idea.
How could you find the kittens?
How would YOU solve this problem?

Here's another problem!

An airplane has landed on top of this building.
The pilot doesn't want to think about this problem.
He just wants to go home.
He knows he's going to have more problems today.

Mei Lin thinks she has a way to solve the problem.
She says "Why not get a big helicopter –
it can lift this little plane off the roof.
Maybe that will solve the problem?"
The pilot says "Bah!"

But some people think that might work.
Andy has an idea, too.

"What we need are people with tools.
They can take the airplane apart.
Then we can carry the airplane down the stairs . . .
piece by piece, by piece, by piece, by piece."

Some people say, "Hmmm. Interesting idea."
The pilot just groans.

Then Wild Wally has an idea.
"I have solved the problem!
Why don't we all get together
and just push the airplane off the roof!
That will get rid of the airplane a lot faster."
The pilot starts to cry.

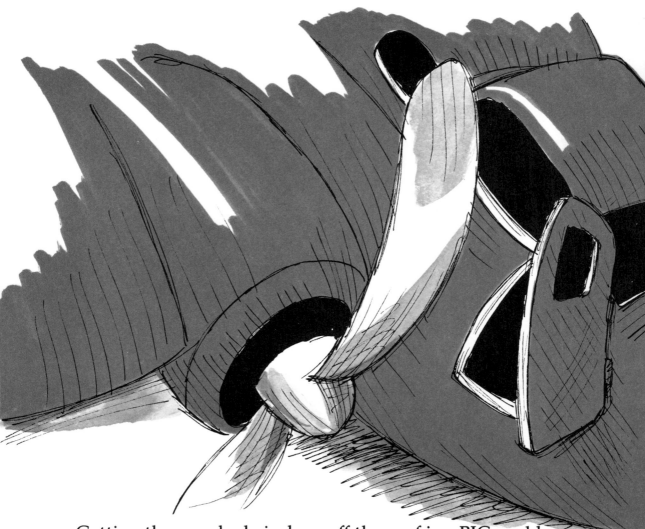

Getting the wrecked airplane off the roof is a BIG problem.
Mei Lin, Andy, and Wild Wally have come up with
three different ways of SOLVING the problem.

What is good about Mei Lin's way?
What might go wrong with it?

What is good about Andy's way?
What might go wrong with it?

What is good about Wild Wally's way?
What might go wrong with it?

Do YOU have an idea for
getting the wrecked airplane off the roof?
Can you think of a way to solve the problem?

What is good about your way?
What might go wrong with it?

You must be getting good at solving problems by now.
Here is a tough one.

What if you were on your way to the store
to buy some groceries for your mom
and you were almost there,
and there was this puddle in the street,
and this huge truck came along, and . . . .

SPLAT!
You are drenched with mud!
You are yucky with mud!
You are covered with horrible, dirty street mud!
Blech!

What are you going to do?
How are you going to solve this problem?

Maybe you could run back home,
change your clothes, and start all over again.
But you're almost to the store,
and it's a LONG way back home . . . .

Maybe you should go to a friend's house
and ask if you could clean up.
But your friend lives three blocks away.
And suppose she's not home?

Maybe you should go on your way,
mud and all.
But suppose the people at the store laugh at you?
And they might not let you in
because you are covered with mud!

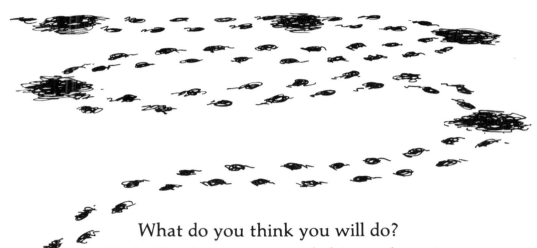

What do you think you will do?
Each idea has some good things about it.
But each idea has some bad things about it, too.
What do you think is the best idea?
Why do you think it is the best way to solve the problem?
Do you think another way would be better?

Sometimes it's hard to know which way
is the best way to solve a problem.

Kamala has a best friend.
His name is William.
Kamala and William go everywhere together.
They are always laughing together.

But today William is crying.
William doesn't usually cry.
Kamala doesn't like to see him cry.
She hopes that she can help him.

"What's the matter?" asks Kamala.
"Nothing," says William.
"What's making you cry?" asks Kamala.
"Go away," says William sadly.

Kamala wants to help William with his troubles.
But William won't tell her what is bothering him.
How can Kamala help him?
Kamala has a problem.

Kamala thinks of some ways to solve her problem.

She could talk to William's other good friend, Max.
Maybe Max knows why William is feeling so sad.

She could go speak to William's mom and dad.
They might know what is troubling William.

She could keep on asking William what the trouble is.
Maybe if she asks him enough times, William will tell her.

She could spend a lot more time with William
and be extra nice to him.
That might make him feel better . . .
even if she NEVER finds out what made him cry.

Suppose your friend was feeling very sad.
Here are some things for you to think about.

What are some good ways I can think of to solve this problem?

Which way will solve the problem best?

Which way is fastest?

Which way is easiest?

What might go wrong?

You need to practice being a good problem solver.
Some problems are easy to solve.

"Carl needs to cross a busy street . . . ."

Some problems are very hard:

"Gina saw people throwing wrappers and bottles
and newspapers all over the park.
She wants to find a way to keep the park clean . . . ."

Can you figure out a way to keep people from littering?

How would you solve this problem?